English Furniture of the Eighteenth Century

By

Frederick Litchfield

British Library Cataloguing-in-Publication Data
A catalogue record for this book is available from
the British Library

late century introduced the 'Aesthetic movement' (essentially promoting the beauty of objects above any other social or political themes) and the 'Arts and Crafts movement' (An international design movement that flourished between 1860-1910, led by William Morris. It stood for traditional craftsmanship using simple form, often applying medieval, romantic or folk styles of decoration). Art Nouveau, in turn was influenced by both of these movements. This latter development was perhaps the most influential of all, inspired by natural forms and structures; evident primarily in architecture, but also the beautiful objects crafted to fill such spaces. Noted furniture designers in this style included William H. Bradley; the 'Dean of American Designers', Goerges de Feure, the Parisian designer who famously produced the theatre designs for *Le Chat Noir* cabaret, and Hermann Obrist, a German sculptor of the Jugendstil (the German branch of Art Nouveaux) movement.

The first three-quarters of the twentieth century are often seen as the march towards Modernism in furniture design. Modernism, in general, includes the activities and creations of those who felt traditional forms of art, architecture, literature, religious faith and social activities were becoming outdated in the new economic, social, and political environment of an emergent industrialized world. Art Deco, De Stijl, Bauhaus, Wiener Werkstätte, and Vienna Secession designers all worked to some degree within the Modernist idiom. Born from the Bauhaus and Art Deco/Streamline styles came the post WWII 'Mid-Century Modern' style using materials developed during the war including laminated plywood, plastics and fibreglass. Prime examples include furniture designed by George Nelson Associates, Charles and Ray Eames, Paul McCobb and Danish modern designers including Finn Juhl and Arne Jacobsen. Post-modern design, intersecting the Pop art movement, gained steam in the 1960s and 70s, promoted in the 1980s by groups such as the Italy-based Memphis movement. The latter group worked with ephemeral designs, featuring colourful decoration and asymmetrical shapes.

As is evident from this short history, the history of artistic developments is inextricably linked with the progression of furniture design. This is hardly surprising, as after all, many artists, thinkers and designers would stringently resist any artificial separation between traditional fine art and functional design. Both respond to their wider context and environment, both, perhaps in differing ways, seeking to impact on reality and society.

Today, British professional furniture makers have self organised into a strong and vibrant community, largely under the organisation 'The Worshipful Company of Furniture Makers', commonly referred to as the Furniture Makers or the Furniture Makers Company. Its motto is 'Straight and Strong'! Members of the Company come from many professions and disciplines, but the common link is that all members on joining must be engaged in or with the UK furnishing industry. Thus the work of the Company is delivered by members with wide ranging professional knowledge and skills in manufacturing, retailing, education, journalism; in fact any aspect of the industry. There are many similar organisations across the globe, as well as in the UK, all seeking to integrate and promote the valuable art that is furniture making. Education is a key factor in such endeavours, and maintaining strong links between professional practitioners, didactic colleges and the amateur maker/restorer is crucial. We hope the reader enjoys this book.

Contents

The term Georgian—Dutch influence on English furniture, the use of mahogany—Gillow established. THOMAS CHIPPENDALE—Early work—"The Cabinet Maker and Director"—Influence of Sir W. Chambers—Chippendale's second period—The Society of Upholders and Cabinet makers—Chippendale's designs. HAIG AND CHIPPENDALE—An old account quoted. INCE AND MAYHEW—Their book of designs. CONTEMPORARY MANU-FACTURERS—Thomas Johnson, Mathias Lock, Manwaring. A HEPPELWHITE AND CO.—Book of designs and list of patterns—Influence of Robert and James Adam. GILLOWS—Popular fancies. THOMAS SHERATON—"The Cabinet maker and Up-holsterer's drawing book"—Designer rather than Manufacturer—Some particulars of his career—His designs and criticisms on his contemporaries. PAINTED AND ENAMELLED FURNITURE—The Adam influence—Contemporary artists who painted fur-niture—Wedgwood's plaques inserted—Process of finishing painted furniture—Old and new work—Museum references.

I T is a curious instance of the whirligig of fashion that the term "Georgian," which thirty years ago was applied to architecture and clumsy and massive buildings, affecting the classic style of the ancient temple, but lacking its proportions and dignity, should lately have become a term to denote a fashionable period of taste. The word was one of reproach and contempt, as if to say, making a vulgar pretence, "Georgian!" Now we have rooms, chimney-pieces and furniture, advertised and recommended as "Georgian," by which it is meant that they are of the time including the reigns

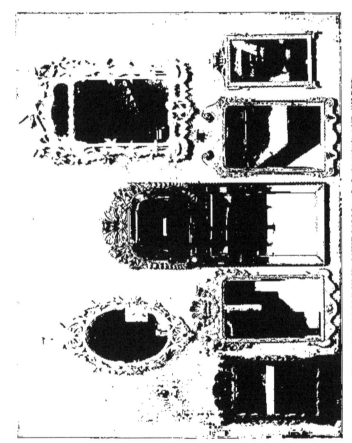

ENGLISH MIRRORS IN WALNUT WOOD, ALSO CARVED AND GILDED
EARLY EIGHTEENTH CENTURY

of the four successive English kings, from 1714 to 1827, and therefore the period of the history of furniture which covers the careers of Chippendale, his contemporaries and immediate successors.

In the chapter on Dutch furniture I have endeavoured to show that at the end of the seventeenth, and during the early part of the eighteenth century, that is, from the accession of William and Mary to the death of Queen Anne, a strong Dutch influence was impressed upon our English furniture. To this time belong the early specimens of our "grandfather" clocks, the old-fashioned bureau-bookcase, the chair with cabriole leg and claw-and-ball foot, and a flat-shaped "splat" in the back; mirrors with narrow walnut-wood moulded frames, the larger ones having the glass in two or three divisions, chests of drawers inclosed by two doors of walnut wood, veneered in patterns formed by the figure of the wood running different ways, and such smaller articles as the tripod stand for a basin, and the work table fitted with contrivances for winding silks, and other ladies' accessories: the harpsichord and spinet, the quaint card table with cabriole leg, sometimes ornamented with an eagle's head; and English lacquer made in imitation of that which originally came from China and Japan. These form a rough list of some of the articles of furniture about this time.

The use of mahogany was becoming fashionable, for, although discovered as a rare wood more than a hundred years previously, it was not until the first quarter of the eighteenth century had turned, that it was extensively used in the manufacture of furniture. The house of Gillow was founded in Lancaster at the end of the seventeenth century, although the London branch was not opened until 1765, and this firm's reputation for well-made solid mahogany furniture was then established.

Thomas Chippendale

It is difficult to assign any precise date to the first work of Thomas Chippendale. There is a chair in the Soane Museum, said to be the work of his own hand, and the original receipt for payment is stated to have once been in the possession of the museum. This is of the Dutch type, to which reference has already been made, and the date one would put at about 1720. There is also the illustration of a chair in "The Furniture of our Ancestors," which the author tells us was brought to England in 1727, and this has every appearance of being by Chippendale, and we know that the first edition of the famous "Gentleman and Cabinetmaker's Director" was published by him in 1754. Mrs. R. S. Clouston, who has written several articles for "The Connoisseur" on this famous furniture designer and maker, thinks that his first work may have been done as early as 1715.

When we consider that the date of the publication of the third edition of the "Director" was in 1762, he would have been about seventy years of age at this time if any work of his was *en évidence* in 1715. I am inclined, therefore, to place the date of his first work somewhat later, say from 1720-1725.

Chippendale, who was a native of Worcestershire, established himself as a cabinet maker in St. Martin's Lane, probably somewhere about 1720-1725, and at first made the kind of chairs which

ENGLISH SETTEE IN WALNUT
EARLY EIGHTEENTH CENTURY (CHIPPENDALE'S FIRST PERIOD)

CHAIR ATTRIBUTED TO CHIPPENDALE

CHAIR BY THOMAS CHIPPENDALE

6

I have already alluded to, more Dutch than English in character, but of mahogany instead of walnut, which the Dutch more generally used. His second period seems to have derived its inspiration from Sir William Chambers, R.A., the architect of Somerset House, who about this time, 1745-1750, had travelled in the East and returned imbued with strong impressions of Chinese designs, which he introduced to his clients. He published a book, entitled "Chinese Buildings," in 1757, and built the Pagoda in Kew Gardens. Chinese pagodas, Chinese wall-papers and designs became a fashion, and Chippendale, who was more adapter than original designer, made his chairs and mirror frames to suit the rooms designed by Chambers. In several of the houses of Sackville Street, Dublin, and also in other parts of that city, there are still evidences of this combination; on the walls of the staircase and over the chimney-piece there is a panel inclosed by a rococo frame of stucco work, part of the original design of the house, and such panels could really have had no other suitable filling than one of Chippendale's rococo frames.

In the "Director" there are several designs for these, with a Chinese mandarin holding an umbrella on the top, and some quaint stork-like birds perched on conventional rockwork with dripping water. The frame is divided into several compartments by rococo scrolls and bevelled-sided little pilasters.

The chairs and some of the cabinets followed similar lines. The upper part of the cabinets are in imitation of a Chinese joss-house, and some of the chairs have an Eastern lattice for the back, finishing at the top with a carved ornament resembling the roof of a pagoda.

Some years later we find that, taking fresh impressions from the lighter style of the French furniture of the time, that is, the more frivolous curves and scrolls of the Louis XV period, Chippendale made his chairs of more fanciful patterns, like the riband-backed design which is so well known and so frequently copied. To many of the drawings in his third edition of the " Director " we find the description "a French commode," or similar title, which shows that in following the prevailing fashion, Chippendale was adapting some of his new designs to French patterns.

In another book published about this time, and containing the reproductions of several of Chippendale's drawings, there is the following inscription on the title-page: "Upwards of one hundred new and genteel designs, being all the most approved patterns of household furniture in the French taste. By a Society of Upholders and Cabinet makers." This title-page bears no date, but it is said that Chippendale was formerly a member of the society, and after some disagreement, decided to publish his own book of designs independently. Within the last few years there have been published cheap reproductions of the original books, and readers can see for themselves the strong French bent which the ornamental furniture of this time was now taking.

Chippendale's furniture has been much criticised on account of the fanciful details of many of his designs, but some of the criticisms would lose much of their force if the articles of furniture, either made by him or by the best of his contemporaries, were before the critics, instead of only the designs. It is said that Chippendale handed his original draw-

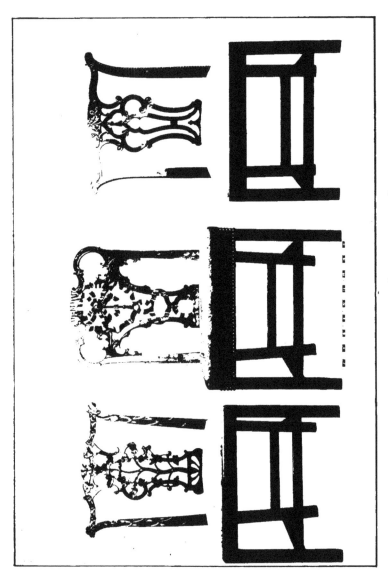

CHIPPENDALE CHAIRS (SECOND PERIOD)

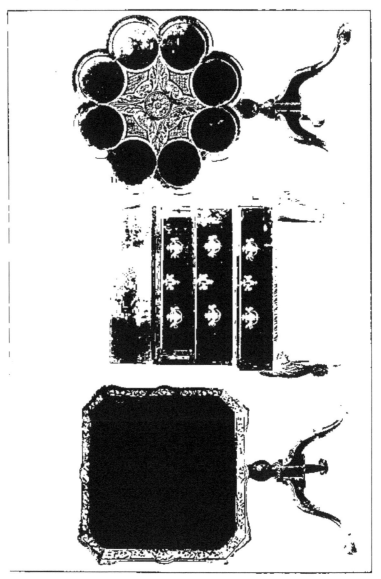

THREE PIECES OF FURNITURE ATTRIBUTED TO CHIPPENDALE

12

ings to the copperplate engraver, who would naturally endeavour to make his work as artistic as possible, and in so doing, while producing a charming design, rendered it scarcely practicable for a cabinet or chair maker, by reason of the fineness of the lines and consequent absence of strength and solidity. In really good old furniture by the best makers of this time, there is in the well-moulded sweep of the curves, some compensation for the apparent fragility of design, and in the chapter on "faked furniture" and in "Hints and Cautions" I have endeavoured to point out one of the signs by which the real old chair or frame may be distinguished from the imitation. It is this "sweep" which requires so much more wood, and consequently infinitely more skilful work. A chair frame which is apparently only two inches thick must be cut from mahogany of some four or five inches substance, to allow for the sweep in the lines of a good old Chippendale chair—but more of this has been said in the chapters already referred to, and we must return to the books of designs. There are several names of articles of furniture which are now but interesting links with the past: "Library case" instead of bookcase; "Bar-backed sofa," the settee of the period formed like three or four chairs placed side by side, with an arm at either end; "Confidante" or "Duchesse," the former being the two-chair settee of the time, and the latter the English equivalent of a French *chaise-longue*; "Tea chest" and "urn stand," which remind us of the time when tea was an expensive luxury, costing 10s. and 12s. a pound. The urn stand was a charming little table, sometimes oval and sometimes square on four tapering legs, with a little slide pulling out underneath its top to accommodate the teapot, which was filled from the urn. These are a few of the names of the two hundred designs in Chippendale's book.

The full-page illustrations of specimens of Chippendale's furniture selected from those in the South Kensington collection, will demonstrate the different periods of his work, the earlier chairs showing the Dutch and then the Chinese influences, while the later ones show the lighter and more capricious lines which were adopted from the French fashions.

Haig and Chippendale

By the kindness of Captain Herbert Terry of Ripley, an enthusiastic collector of old English furniture, I am able to give an illustration from a photograph of the first and last pages of an original bill receipted by Thomas Chippendale, junior, who had at this time a partner, the firm being Haig and Chippendale. The whole account, consisting of several folios, is for the furnishing of the town house of Sir Richard Frederick, who was Captain Terry's great-uncle, and the document has been in the possession of the family ever since it was rendered. As the photograph indicates, it was commenced in 1790, and the balance paid in 1796, and it includes a great many very ordinary household items, by no means of the ornamental kind that we are in the habit of associating with the name of Chippendale. On reference to the old London Directories in the newspaper room of the British Museum, there will be found the name of the firm described as "upholders and cabinet makers" of 60, St. Martin's Lane, Charing Cross,

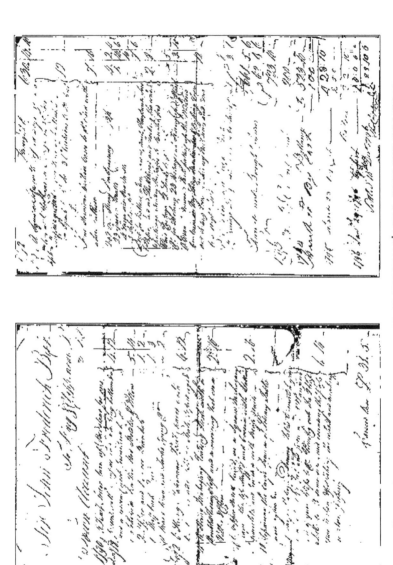

THE FIRST AND LAST PAGES OF HAIG AND CHIPPENDALE'S BILL, WITH THE SIGNATURE
OF THOMAS CHIPPENDALE

from 1790 to 1798, when the name of Thomas Chippendale, "cabinet maker" of the same address, appears alone, from which it is evident that either Haig died, or that the partnership had been dissolved. It is singular that the name of Haig should precede that of Chippendale, as if he were at the time senior partner, and it may be that the original Thomas, like so many men who did excellent work, died in circumstances that rendered it advisable that the son who succeeded him should seek the pecuniary assistance of a partner with capital to enable him to carry on the business, and that after the father's death the character of the business became less of a special, and more of a general furnishing character. We can only guess, but the account quoted above, rather leads one to this conclusion.

The prices charged for some of the articles afford material for interesting comparison with those which such things would realize at the present time. While on the subject of prices, however, it should be mentioned that it is only within the last twenty years that Chippendale furniture has appreciated at such a rapid rate. Twenty-five years ago, excellent Chippendale, Heppelwhite or Sheraton chairs could have been bought for ten pounds each, and the more ordinary kinds for twenty-five to thirty-five shillings each.

The following is an extract from the above mentioned account of Haig and Chippendale.

	£	s.	d.
A very large mahogany wardrobe of good wood for the recess with folding doors and 7 slideing shelves lin'd with marble paper and baize aprons 2 long and 2 short drawers under	16	10	0

	£	s.	d.
A large oval work table with folding top made of fine black rosewood banded with white a drawer in front, and therm feet in strong socket castors	5	16	0
A large Wainscot press bedstead with folding doors and sacking bottom for nursery	3	10	0
12 neat carv'd Mahogany square back Parlor chairs the seats stuffed and covered with the finest green Morocco leather and finished with double rows of best gilt nails 48*s*. ea.	28	16	0
6 ditto arm'd chairs seats stuffed and cover'd in the same manner 58*s*.	17	8	0

It is worth while to note some points in the above extract. One of these is, that from the wording of the first item it is evident that "good" wood was then, as now, an appreciable quality; it occurs in other items in the bill, and proves that there was then, as now, "good," bad and indifferent, and that not everything that is old was necessarily made of good, that is, carefully selected and well-figured material.

In the second item, the work table is described as being made of "fine black rosewood." In 1803 Sheraton mentions this "black" rosewood as being the fashion, and therefore we may assume that somewhere about 1790, or a little earlier, this wood was in favour for a certain class of ornamental furniture. The "therm" feet are doubtless the tapered form supports which came in about this time, after the cabriole or scroll-form leg had gone out of fashion. On the first page of the bill, which is illustrated from a photograph, some chairs are described as having tapered legs. The set of eighteen "parlor" chairs, twelve single and six arms, have also an interest, as marking the time when these square-framed chairs with upholstered backs came into vogue, and if we turn to one of the illustrations of Sheraton's designs, this kind of chair will be seen. It is quite evident, then, that Haig and Chippendale conformed, like most other manufacturers, to the fashions of the day, which altered between 1780 and 1790 to the more sedate and sober lines which are

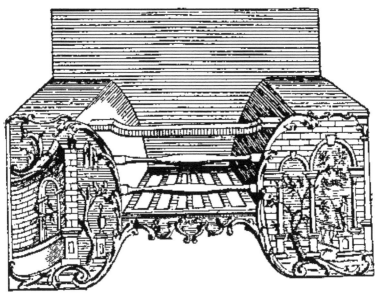

A BATH STOVE, BY INCE AND MAYHEW

generally associated with the names of Sheraton and Heppelwhite.

Captain Terry's brother still has in his possession the wardrobe for which the sum of £16 10s. was charged in this account.

Ince and Mayhew

Another firm that carried on an extensive business about the same period as Thomas Chippendale was Ince and Mayhew, in Broad Street, Golden Square, who also published a book of designs, entitled "The Cabinet maker's real friend and companion." It is singular that while the imprint on some old copper-plates in my possession should

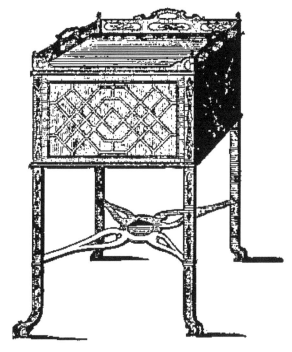

A BEDROOM TABLE, BY INCE AND MAYHEW

be "Ince and Mayhew," with the address given as above, and while Sheraton in criticising their book of designs should write of the firm as it is here named, yet in the old London Directories of 1791-1795, and also in the list of master cabinet makers given by Sheraton at the end of his "Cabinet Dictionary," published in 1803, the style

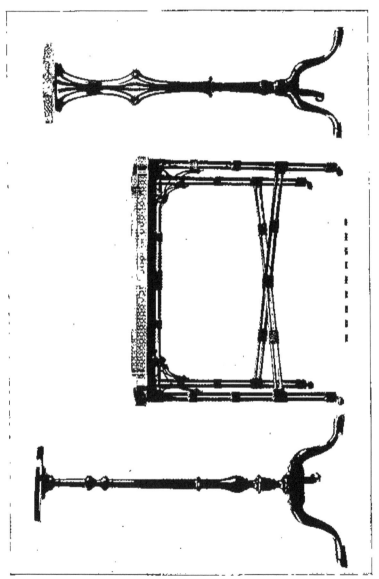

TABLE AND LAMP STANDS ATTRIBUTED TO INCE AND MAYHEW

of the firm should be Mayhew and Ince, and the address Marshall Street, Carnaby Market.

The designs published by them are similar to

A BEDROOM TABLE, BY INCE AND MAYHEW

those of Chippendale, but have more of the fret-cut ornament than we find in the drawings of the latter. Indeed, although this fret-cut work has been so commonly identified with Chippendale there is remarkably little of it in his book.

The three illustrations in the text of designs by Ince and Mayhew, will show that, but for the fact of their appearance in the book of designs published by them, it would be somewhat difficult to "place" them. The Bath stove, although perhaps scarcely within the strict limits of furniture, has been selected because it shows the "baroque" taste of this period. The bedroom table, on the other hand, has more of the fret-cut ornament which has just been alluded to, while the bedroom table is quite of the Chippendale character in the scroll leg and also in the ornamental framing of the panel.

Contemporary Manufacturers

Some of the other manufacturers of this time, whose names are scarcely known now, but who nevertheless produced good work, were the following: France, a neighbour of Chippendale's in St. Martin's Lane; Charles Elliott; Campbell and Sons; Thomas Johnson; Copeland; Robert Davy; a celebrated chair-maker named Manwaring, and Mathias Lock. Of these men little is known of France, Elliott, and Campbell, save that they held appointments as cabinet makers to the King, the Prince of Wales and the Duke of York, but of Mathias Lock, Copeland, and Johnson, there is more information available.

Thomas Johnson was a carver who carried on business in Queen Street, near Seven Dials, Holborn, and published several books of designs for furniture. His first work, entitled "Twelve Girandoles," appeared in 1755, and his second in 1758 contained a number of drawings of chairs still more flamboyant than those of Chippendale.

ENGLISH FURNITURE
LATE EIGHTEENTH CENTURY

Mrs. R. S. Clouston's contention that we can trace Chippendale's more rococo style, which is evident in the second edition of his " Director," published in 1759, to the influence of Johnson's work of the previous year, may be correct.

Mathias Lock also published designs, both separately and in collaboration with Copeland, and as some of his original drawings are preserved in the South Kensington Library, they are available for examination. There are also some interesting memoranda attached to them, from which it appears that five shillings a day was at that time the full wage of a skilful wood-carver.

Manwaring also published a book which contained his designs for chairs, similar to Chippendale's, but with some technical differences, and as Mrs. Clouston has so carefully investigated them it is only fair to quote from her article in the " Connoisseur " of March, 1904 : " The method in which the top rail joins itself to the design of the splat, the plain square leg in conjunction with a carved back, the bracket and the shaped front, would each of them have been unlikely in Chippendale's work, but are all typical of Manwaring."

A. Heppelwhite and Co.

Towards the latter part of Chippendale's time, *i.e.*, in 1789, the firm of A. Heppelwhite and Co. published a book of designs.

This valuable work of reference contains a hundred and twenty-seven copperplates with three hundred drawings of furniture, and is entitled " The Cabinet maker and Upholsterer's Guide, etc." So little attention comparatively, has been paid to this designer and manufacturer of late eighteenth-century furniture, by writers on the subject, that it may be of some service to the reader to quote the list of patterns illustrated:

"Chairs
Stools
Sofas
Confidante
Duchesse
Side-boards
Pedestals and Vases
Cellerets
Commodes
Rudd's table
Bidets
Night tables
Bason stands
Wardrobes
Bed pillars
Knife cases
Desk and Bookcases
Secretary and Book-
  cases
Library cases
Library tables
Reading desks
Chests of drawers
Urn stands
Pot cupboards

Brackets
Hanging shelves
Fire screens
Beds
Field Beds
Sweeptops for ditto
Tea Caddies
Tea Trays
Card tables
Pier tables
Pembroke tables
Tambour tables
Dressing glasses
Dressing tables and
  drawers
Candle stands
Lamp stands
Pier glasses
Terms for Busts
Cornices for Library
  cases
Wardrobes, etc., at large
Ornamental tops for
  Pier tables, Pembroke
  tables, commodes, etc.

in the plainest and most enriched styles with a scale to each, and an explanation in letterpress."

It will be seen that this is a fairly complete list, and the designs themselves are in excellent taste.

ENGLISH CHAIRS
LATE EIGHTEENTH CENTURY

The lines of chairs and sofas are restrained and dignified, neat but not effeminate, chaste and yet not severe. Where marqueterie is employed as a decoration, it is as a rich border to a plain centre, or an oval centre fan ornament with a festoon of husks or drapery. The drawings show that Heppelwhite was careful to use richly-figured veneers

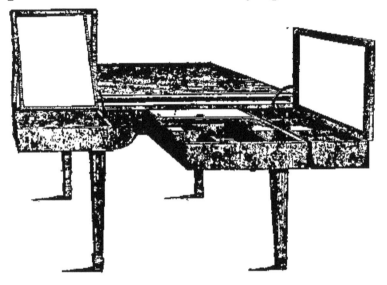

"RUDD'S TABLE," BY A. HEPPELWHITE

for his tables, wardrobes or bookcases, and other pieces having plain surfaces.

The illustration given above of Rudd's table, or "a reflecting dressing table" is fully described in Heppelwhite's book, as taking its name from a "once popular character" for whom it was first made, and will convey to the reader an excellent idea of the mechanical tables in fashion at this period.

Generally speaking, one sees that the furniture

of Heppelwhite was designed for the houses built by Robert and James Adam, who at this time were designing some of the London streets, which remain as testimony of the good taste which marked their work. Stratford Place, part of Fitzroy Square, Adelphi Terrace, parts of Portman Square, Portland Place, and other important thoroughfares, can still be identified by the refined treatment of exterior as well as interior decoration.

Besides the furniture of mahogany, solid and

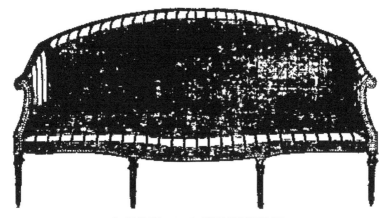

A COUCH, BY A. HEPPELWHITE

veneered, and of satinwood and marqueterie, Heppelwhite also devoted considerable attention to making furniture in beech and birch woods for enamelling and painting, and in his book directions are given as to the best kind of covering for such furniture.

Some chairs by this maker are in the Victoria and Albert Museum, and are reproduced in the full-page illustrations of this chapter. Some of the smaller illustrations given in the text have been selected as showing a few of the many designs in his book.

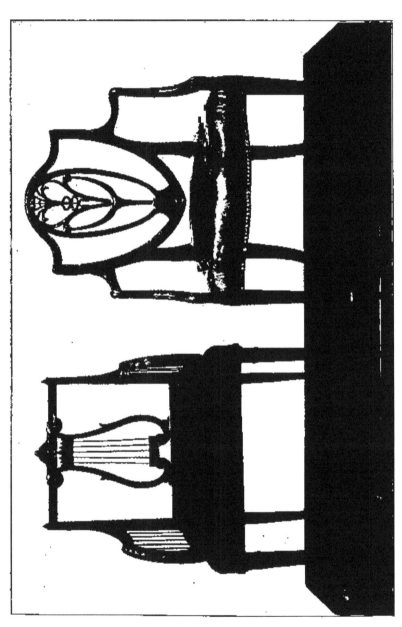

CHAIRS ATTRIBUTED TO HEPPELWHITE

34

The couch illustrated on page 84 is in every respect an adaptation of a French Louis Seize design, while the window seat and the screens are dainty pieces of decorative furniture, characteristic of the period and the style of this firm.

The "eared armchair" was made by many other upholsterers and cabinet makers of the period, and under the title of a "grandfather's chair," has been much reproduced during the present revival of the taste for old English furniture.

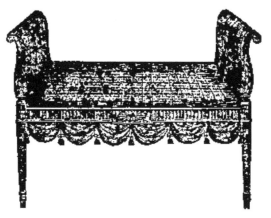

A WINDOW SEAT, BY A. HEPPELWHITE

A. Heppelwhite and Co. style themselves cabinet makers on the title-page of their book, but it is curious that the name does not appear in the London directories of the time, and still more strange that, in what purports to be a complete list of master cabinet makers and kindred trades compiled by Thomas Sheraton and placed at the end of the "Cabinet Dictionary," which he published in 1803, the name of this firm is not included. Thomas Chippendale, Robert Gillow and Co., Mayhew and Ince, Snell, Seddon and Co., and a great many

others are there, but not Heppelwhite. It almost
seems as if they were like Sheraton himself, more
theoretical than practical; or they may have worked
exclusively for architects such as the Adams, and

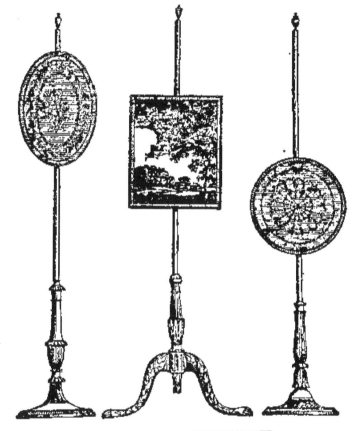

POLE SCREENS BY HEPPELWHITE

had no regular show-room for the public. Unlike
Chippendale's book, which gives his address, and
also includes in the preface certain personal state-
ments as to his ability to carry out any of the
designs illustrated, the Heppelwhites give no

address, nor is there a single sentence which indicates a desire to secure increased trade by the publication of their designs.

The omission of the name in the directory I attach less importance to, than that from Sheraton's list, because the "London Directory" of the years referred to are very thin books of not much over half an inch thickness, and include what the compiler terms "eminent" bankers, merchants, and tradesmen, and many names in Sheraton's list are not to be found amongst the "eminent" ones of the directories.

Gillows

It should be remembered that at this period "Gillows" were carrying on a large business, and no doubt altered their designs to the new fashion. As a proof of this I may give an instance. Messrs. Waring and Gillow, who some few years ago acquired the business of the original firm of Gillows, lately exhibited a wardrobe which they stated to be an exact reproduction of one made by the old firm in the year 1796. The piece in question was of rich mahogany with broad bandings of satinwood, and was in every way just one of those which would be termed by nine persons out of ten a "Sheraton" design.

I think it was Mr. Balfour who in his manifesto on the great tariff controversy said, that "the British public like labels." This is quite as true of commodities as it is of political "war cries," and when once a certain class of furniture comes to be known by any given characteristics, it must be by the particular maker or of that particular kind, or it counts for nothing with the public. Thus it is that

every piece of old mahogany furniture is labelled
" Chippendale," and by the same sort of rule every
piece with satinwood inlay is called " Sheraton."
The truth surely is, that when a fashionable craze
sets in, it is followed, more or less, by all the manu-
facturers, but as only a few names become popular,
these better-known makers have credit for a great
deal of work which has been done by others.

Thomas Sheraton

Next to Chippendale the name most familiar
to the ordinary buyer or collector of old English
furniture, is that of Thomas Sheraton. He was
apparently a well-educated man, but from the
rather didactic phraseology of " The Cabinet
Maker and Upholsterer's Drawing Book," which
was published by him in 1793, one gathers that
he was a man who had risen from the ranks, and
prided himself on his self-acquired knowledge.
That he was an excellent draughtsman is without
doubt, and in a rather verbose lecture on the laws
of geometry and the five orders of architecture, he
claimed to base all his designs on geometrical
science. The book contains elaborate directions
for perspective drawing, and his diagrams are as
carefully finished as an engineer's plans, drawn to
scale with mathematical nicety and precision.

How far he himself carried out his own designs
is not known, nor have I been able to ascertain
where he carried on business. When I was engaged in writing my " Illustrated History of Furniture," Mr. Black, of the publishing firm of
A. and C. Black, Soho Square, told me that his
grandfather, Mr. Adam Black, had, when quite a

young man, assisted Sheraton in the production of his book, and that at the time the famous designer was in such poor circumstances, as to be obliged to raise money by giving drawing lessons.

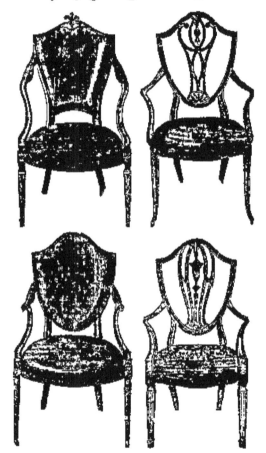

"SHIELD BACK" CHAIRS, DESIGNED BY SHERATON OR HEPPELWHITE

From this it is pretty evident that he must have been in a very small way of business, and it will probably be somewhat of a shock to many amateurs of old English furniture, to learn that Sheraton was chiefly a designer and draughtsman. He was also a zealous Baptist, and published several books and pamphlets advocating his religious views. Besides his "Drawing Book" he also published in 1803 "The Cabinet Dictionary," explaining all the terms used by the "cabinet, chair, and upholsterers' branches," and he was engaged on "The Cabinet Maker and Artists' Encyclopaedia" when he died in 1806 in Broad Street, Soho, leaving his family in distressed circumstances.

As regards the designs of his chairs, they are practically so similar to many of those of Heppelwhite, that unless we had their respective books for identification it would be impossible to tell the one from the other. Both include the "shield" back with the Prince of Wales's feather ornament, and those with drapery festoons and "vase" centres. The Prince of Wales's feather, by the way, indicated something besides mere decoration; it was the badge of the young Court party as led by the Prince of Wales, afterwards George IV.

The designs of Sheraton's marqueterie were somewhat similar to those of Heppelwhite, chiefly composed of mahogany and satinwood, but he depended more upon the excellent choice of his veneers, than upon elaborate ornament for his effects. His drawings indicate this, because the figure of the wood is shown by shaded lines. A characteristic feature of his cabinet designs, was the graceful "swan-necked" pediment surmounting the cornice of wardrobe, bookcase or cabinet. The sideboard of mahogany, banded with satinwood having fan pattern ornaments inlaid, the ends being rounded, supported by tapering legs, is a very familiar design, and also the handsome brass rails which were fixed at the back and held a silk curtain to serve as a background to the silver, or ornaments standing on the board. Some of these brass rails were very handsome and supported a circular convex mirror in the centre, also branches for candles. Of the two urns which stood on the sideboard, one contained the silver-mounted knives, forks and spoons for use, and the other

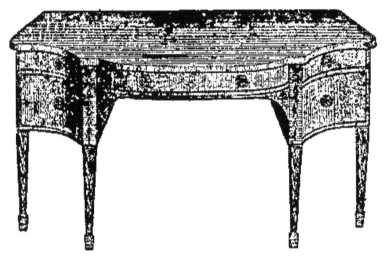

A SIDE TABLE DESIGNED BY T. SHERATON, ABOUT 1795. SHOW-
ING THE WELL-CHOSEN VENEERS, WITH BUT A SLIGHT INLAY
OF BANDING AND THE "HUSK" ORNAMENT

was fitted with a tap and held water for cleansing them—this operation being apparently carried on in the room while the family was at dinner. They are graceful accessories, and were beautifully made, the alternate flutings of mahogany and satinwood being very carefully finished. Instead of these urns, knife cases were sometimes, or rather more generally, used. Most collectors know these quaintly-shaped boxes, made in mahogany or satinwood, inlaid with shell ornaments, and of late years converted into spirit cases or holders for stationery.

Sheraton also designed a great many of the mechanical tables fashionable at the time. "A cylinder wash-hand table," besides the circular revolving front from which it derives its name, and which concealed the basin when shut, had a toilet glass which rose with a spring and a catch. From the sides were drawn out a bidet and water drawer. Some of his reading and writing tables had a number of adjustable slides and drawers with neatly contrived fittings.

The preface of his book contains severe strictures upon the want of perspective in the drawings of Chippendale and Heppelwhite, and particularly of those published by the "Society of Cabinet makers in London," to which it is thought that Chippendale, Manwaring, Johnson and others belonged.

By the light of recent events, when a couple of chairs by Chippendale have been sold at Christie's for a thousand guineas, it is amusing to quote Sheraton on page 9 of the preface of a book written within, say, ten or fifteen years of his rival's death. "Chippendale's book has, it is true, given us the proportion of the Five Orders, and lines for two or three cases, which is all it pretends to, relative to rules for drawing; *and as for the designs themselves, they are now wholly antiquated and laid aside,* though possessed of great merit, according to the times in which they were executed."

Then, dealing with the designs of Ince and Mayhew, he says, "The designs in cabinets and chairs are of course of the same cast, and have therefore suffered the same fate (been wholly laid

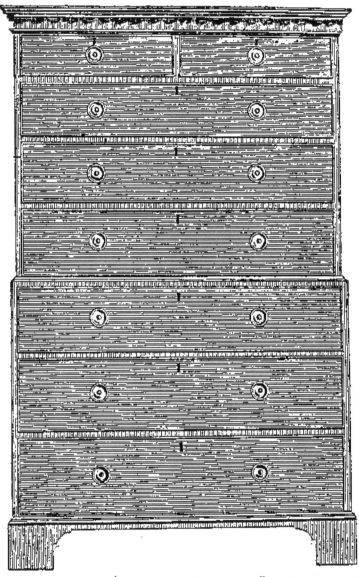

DOUBLE CHEST OF DRAWERS OR "TALL BOY," ABOUT THE END OF THE EIGHTEENTH CENTURY, MADE BY SEVERAL MANU-FACTURERS (included in Heppelwhite's designs)

aside), in the cabinet branch according to the present taste, yet in justice to the work it may be said to have been a book of merit in its day, though inferior to Chippendale's, which was a real original, as well as more masterful and extensive in its designs."

Of Sheraton's later work from 1800 until his death six years afterwards, something will be said in the following chapter. He caught the fashionable epidemic of the Napoleonic fashion, and some of his bad English copies of the First Empire patterns do not enhance his reputation as a designer. In my "Illustrated History of Furniture" I have been able to give a much larger selection both from his and from Heppelwhite's designs than the limited space admits in this work. Both men have left their mark upon the furniture of English design and manufacture of the time corresponding to the period of Marie Antoinette in France. They show a similar spirit of grace and refinement, a relief from the *baroque* and flamboyant styles of Chippendale and his school, which corresponded to the rococo taste prevalent in France during the latter part of the reign of Louis XV.

Painted and Enamelled Furniture

The decoration of furniture by painting and enamelling, came into fashion in England during the latter part of the eighteenth century. Suites of chairs and sofas to match, made of beech or birch wood, were after careful preparation coated with successive layers of paint, white, cream colour, green and also black, and on these different

ENGLISH SATINWOOD COMMODE WITH PAINTED DECORATION
END OF THE EIGHTEENTH CENTURY

ground colours, panels of scrolls, figure subjects, landscapes and flowers were painted. The lines which defined the panels, and also such prominent parts of the chair as the terminals of the arms and feet, were gilt. The figure subjects in vogue were such as we find in the old Bartolozzi prints or pictures by Angelica Kauffmann; it was a time when the latter artist, Cipriani, Francesco Piranesi, and other contemporary painters were doing excellent work of a decorative character to the order of Robert Adam, who was in the zenith of his fame as an architect.

We have already seen that the brothers Adam were responsible for the interior decoration of many of the houses they designed, as well as the elevations and plans, and this form of enrichment by panel-painting was in great favour. In many old London houses the original work by Kauffmann and her contemporaries still remains, as they were fitted into the stucco panels of the ceilings, and the same kind of decoration was executed for commodes, cabinets, and other articles of furniture. One can call to mind several instances where such original ceilings may still be found, amongst others the house of the Savage Club in Adelphi Terrace, No. 1, Portman Square, and No. 25, Portland Place, designed and built by Robert Adam for his own occupation.

The best decoration by painting was used for such pieces of furniture as were not likely to get much hard wear, and the tops of the half-circular pier tables were favourite subjects for excellent work. In some of these the painting was executed on slabs of copper let into the table tops, while the friezes and legs were gilt, making a very satisfactory combination of colour. The frieze of the table was generally carved in low relief with a design characteristic of the style, either the conventionalized honeysuckle or some other pseudoclassic ornament. The legs tapering, sometimes round and sometimes square, ornamented by flutes with or without husks. Instead of legs a favourite form of support was a pair of griffins, seated, their bodies terminating in scrolls. These mystic animals figured very frequently in Adam's designs, in the upper part of mirror frames, and as standards of tables and cabinets. The commodes of the period, with circular fronts sometimes had the ends concaved while the centre was convex, thus making a graceful serpentine; bookcases had what is termed break-fronts, that is, the long straight line broken by the centre compartment either projecting or receding a couple of inches. Work tables, screens, and other similar articles were made of satinwood or satinwood and mahogany combined, and, with these grounds to show off the painted panels, a very decorative effect was produced.

Another mode of enrichment of this class of furniture was the insertion of plaques of Wedgwood's jasper ware. John Flaxman had been sent to Rome by the great potter, Josiah Wedgwood, to make wax models and drawings of the famous Vatican gems; these were produced by Wedgwood in different colours of jasper ware, and the classical subjects of these plaques, such as the death of Achilles, nymphs sacrificing to Bacchus, and similar mythological illustrations, just suited the furniture of the Adam design and type.

The general lines of design were similar to those of Heppelwhite and Sheraton, and were

PIER TABLE AND WINDOW SEAT BY ROBERT ADAM
END OF THE EIGHTEENTH CENTURY

50

probably in many cases the work of the same cabinet makers, but the decoration was by painting in lieu of marqueterie.

The finishing and polishing of painted furniture required skilful manipulation. The surface of the satinwood or mahogany was first carefully prepared by being scraped, and well rubbed down with sand or glass paper of varying degrees of coarseness, that is, from coarse to fine; then the painter did his work, which naturally stood out in very slight relief. When quite dry and hard, the polisher had to level up with successive coatings of fine white polish, by first treating the unpainted background, and then carefully polishing the whole, giving a glaze and finish to the surface. Sheraton has given us a recipe for making the polish in use at this time, at least some fifty or sixty years before the invention of what is termed "French" polish. Beeswax and turpentine were boiled together, red lead and other colouring matter added if required, and this was applied and well rubbed with a soft pad. Fine brickdust screened by being passed through a stocking, was then "dabbed" on the polished surface, and this was again carefully rubbed to give a fine and uniform dull glaze.

When it was not expedient to employ a good painter for the chief panels, coloured prints were sometimes used, and treated just the same as the hand-painted subjects, by polishing.

English hand-painted furniture differs in one important detail from the *Vernis Martin* French furniture, already described in another chapter. The English work was done either on the wood itself, or on a copper panel let into the wood. In the case of *Vernis Martin*, the panel or surface to be painted was first prepared by successive coatings of the patent varnish invented by the Martins, until a "body" or material was formed which resembled lacquer, the result being similar in effect to that of a highly-finished modern carriage panel.

Beautiful as much of the English painted work is, there is the great disadvantage of its liability to damage by scratches and dents, the result of ordinary wear and use, and such injuries cannot be removed, as is the case with an inlaid marqueterie pattern, but can only be repaired by partially or wholly repainting. It is therefore extremely difficult to find original pieces which do not show signs of more or less successful restoration.

Within the past ten or fifteen years, when the collection of this kind of English work has been fashionable, a number of plain pieces of old furniture suitable for this class of decoration, have been bought, and painted work in the style of the late eighteenth-century artists named above, has been added to enhance the value, and these have found a ready sale.

A great deal of entirely new work, both as to the furniture itself, and also the painting, has been made for the demand which the old work is quite unable to supply. Some of this is carefully done, and although not really old is of a good decorative character, but a great deal is of a cheap and inferior kind, both as to make and finish, and is but a parody on the fine old work which is now so difficult to procure and which realizes an enormous price.

There are some good examples of late eighteenth-century English painted furniture in the

South Kensington Museum, and if the reader should be visiting Ireland he will also find a number of small but representative specimens in the Dublin Museum.

Lightning Source UK Ltd.
Milton Keynes UK
UKHW011303290321
381184UK00002B/656